WHAT OTHERS H

MW01031929

18 Wealth Lessons That \
*Why Prosperity Seldom Taps You on the Shoulder
after Years of Anti-Wealth Programming*

"This wonderful, inspiring book gives you a blueprint for happiness, success, and a good life. You learn that you have no limits to what you can do or achieve."

—**Brian Tracy**
Speaker. consultant, author of more than 80 books

"This is a helpful book for anyone who wants to enhance their thinking and grow their financial security."

—**Nido Qubein**
President, Highpoint University

"Mr. Friedman has taken a long, successful career and distilled it down to the best practices necessary for a successful retirement, and he identifies the pitfalls as well. A simple, must -read roadmap to a comfortable retirement."

—**Frank V. Hibbard**
Mayor, City of Clearwater, Florida

"Mr. Friedman's book is chock-full of wealth lessons that are simple yet powerful—and easy to implement! Everyone should read this book."

—**John Louzonis**
KidsGetRich.com
Author of *Kid Trillionaire:
How a Little Kid Can Make a Big Fortune*

"Get out a highlighter, paper, and pen, and be ready to take notes! Rodger Friedman has successfully synthesized thirty-six years of his wisdom and experience with that of his mentors and teachers to create a compendium of actionable lessons for creating wealth. This book will not only improve your life but those you care about. It's a MUST read!"

—**Dr. David Phelps**
CEO, Freedom Founders
Author of *Own Your Freedom:*
Sustainable Wealth for a Volatile World

"Want to be wealthy? Want to improve your financial life and those of your family? If so, this short book by Rodger Friedman is an excellent read. It's packed with common sense lessons that aren't so common today. No academic theory or wishful thinking, just real, honest-to-goodness practical advice from not only Rodger's own life experiences but also those of his mentors. I enjoyed it immensely and know you will too. Read this book, and then read it again. It's that good!"

—**Jesse S. Lennon III**
President, Pioneer Realty
Real estate entrepreneur, investor, developer, and coach

"Wow! It is not often that a book about wealth takes you through a journey of self-thought and reflection on how to be a better person, citizen, and provider. Rodger's book is a compilation of not only his many years of experience and his desire to spread and share his knowledge and help his fellow men and women, but also a wonderful collection of philosophies and strategies of the masters in wealth accumulation and personal development. This book needs to be on every man, woman, and college graduate's bookshelf and not just read but devoured and acted upon. I cannot wait to purchase a truckload to share with my family, friends, and clients. Thank you for creating this wonderful treasure and sharing it with all of us."

—**Nicholas J Loise**
Past President of GKIC
Founder of Sales Performance Team, LLC

"These pages will likely take you less than one hour to read. However, racing through each of the eighteen chapters without taking time to reflect and honestly respond to the questions and prompts would defeat its true value. I recommend spending time with each chapter, filling in the suggested information, and regularly revisiting the lessons and your responses as you progress toward consistently making smart financial decisions, accumulating greater wealth, and ultimately enjoying your financial freedom."

—**Scott Curtis**
President, Private Client Group, Raymond James

"This is a million-dollar book. It should be read with a pad and pencil nearby. Make sure to take plenty of notes. You will be glad you did!"

—**Keith Cameron Smith**
Entrepreneur and speaker, Author of *The Top 10 Distinctions between Millionaires and the Middle Class*

"Rodger's book *18 Wealth Lessons That Will Transform Your Thinking* is a must-read for all investors and exactly the type of book I recommend to my students and even my own children. Rodger provides practical and sound advice that provides the roadmap toward financial freedom."

—**Brad Thomas**
CEO of Wide Moat Research
Editor of *Forbes Real Estate Investor*
Author of *The Intelligent REIT Investor*

"In this book, Rodger Friedman has presented a reliable and easy-to-understand road map that if acted upon will lead to Wealth and Prosperity. It should be read and the principles it contains memorized by every adult in America. It is mandatory that every young person understand these principles before they get their first check! For the rest of us, it is never too late to learn and apply this knowledge."

—**Gene Kelly**
President and CEO, Accelerated Training Institute

"I read this book in one sitting, and I'm glad I did. I enjoyed Friedman's private stories that lent added personality to the book. Seeing that he had obstacles that he overcame reminded me that implementation trumps ideas anytime. The book is packed with common sense lessons that are not so common today. This book reads like a Chicken Soup for Wealth. His is a voice of experience that speaks volumes and should be listened to."

—**Thomas J. Regan**
Vice President, Group Insurance Sales & Marketing
Metropolitan Life Insurance Company (retired)

"Why is wealth elusive for so many in our great country? Because foundational, true wealth principles are not shared or understood broadly. Even at our most revered higher education institutions there is no "wealth curriculum" or training. It is a shame. You must take control of your wealth and your life. And to do that you must understand the core principles of Wealth. *18 Wealth Lessons That Will Transform Your Thinking* is exactly the right place to start. In this short but powerful book, Rodger Friedman lays out the most important truths about wealth in an easy-to-understand and engaging manner. If you want to change the trajectory of your life, get the book. Read. Decide. Act. Grow."

—**Luke Eddinger**
Managing Director, Robert C. White & Company
and Reven Forest Real Estate

"First, grab a pen, highlighter, or writing weapon of choice. Second, buy a second copy of the book as your first will be filled with notes, comments, plans, and scheming. Finally, here is a book about personal wealth creation/attraction that doesn't drop a bunch of meaningless mumbo-jumbo. The wealthy (aka 1 percenter's) are often vilified for their riches, attacked by the media, and browbeaten by the 99%. Rodger has laid out a step-by-step blueprint that *anyone* can follow to create their version of wealth and autonomy. This book could singlehandedly and exponentially create wealth for thousands if they just take action and implement it. As I always say, You Won't Profit Unless You Implement."

—**Vance Morris**
Founder, Deliver Service Now institute (DSNi)
The *only* Disney service and direct response marketing business on the planet Longest-reigning Marketer of the Year 2015–2019
GKIC International Marketing & Entrepreneur Award

"Finally a book I hold in my hand that reveals the Keys to the Kingdom—the Financial Kingdom protected by a moat few of us get to pass—until now. Be ready for a fresh ride where much of the popular advice given by Big Media is revealed for what it really is. You will come away with the understanding of why the majority is wrong when it comes to building wealth. Follow the steps. My future self is already thanking me for reading this book."

—**Richard Duggal**
"The Closing Machine"
Real Estate Sales Coach

OTHER BOOKS BY RODGER ALAN FRIEDMAN

- **Forging Bonds of Steel**: *How to Build a Successful and Lasting Relationship with Your Financial Advisor*
- **Fire Your Retirement Planner: YOU!** *Concise Advice on How to Join the $100,000 Retirement Club*
- **The Mindset of Retirement Success**: *7 Winning Strategies to Change Your Life*
- **Parent's Guide to Your Child's Retirement**: 21 Thought-Provoking Conversations to Have with Your Adult Children
- **The Iceberg You Don't See**: The Marketing System for Financial Advisors, Co-authored with Parthiv Shah

18 WEALTH LESSONS

THAT WILL TRANSFORM YOUR THINKING

18 WEALTH LESSONS

THAT WILL TRANSFORM YOUR THINKING

WHY PROSPERITY **SELDOM** TAPS YOU ON THE SHOULDER AFTER YEARS —— OF —— **ANTI-WEALTH PROGRAMMING**

IDEA

PLAN

RODGER ALAN FRIEDMAN

Chartered Retirement Planning Counselor SM

Dedicated to Michael Maurer
Rest in peace, my friend

TABLE OF CONTENTS

People are always blaming their circumstances for what they are. I don't believe in circumstances. The people who get on in this world are the people who get up and look for circumstances they want, and if they can't find them, make them.

—GEORGE BERNARD SHAW
British playwright

FOREWORD

Rodgers Friedman's book, **18 Wealth Lessons That Will Transform Your Thinking,** reveals why so many people work a lifetime – earn a living–and when they finally retire, have so little savings to supplement their retirement income, they miss the golden years – and struggle with money worries for the rest of their lives.

This book is not about 'how' to invest. *It is far more valuable.*

Rodger's book is about the BELIEFS, ATTITUDES and BEHAVIORS that empower a small minority of people in this country to retire with enough income to live life comfortably on their own terms. Exactly as they choose. With no money worries. No compromises. And in the style they want to be accustomed to.

The chapters are short. The writing concise. And the stories instructive and memorable.

I enjoyed every page.

Rodger gets to the ROOT CAUSE of why people who have money have it. And why people who struggle with money worries, regardless of how much or how little they earn, struggle.

People who build wealth – and keep enough to live comfortably when they retire – think about MONEY, TIME, SAVING and LIFE differently than others.

They make different decisions than people who retire broke. They have different beliefs about money and time. And because of those beliefs, they develop habits that lead to accomplishment, prosperity, and a well-funded retirement.

Rodger explains it all.

This book is packed with INSIGHT and LESSONS on what people who retire rich, (i.e.: no money worries for the rest of their life), believe about money and what they do different from others who, during their life may earn far more, but retire with far less. Regardless of what you do, how much you earn, or how close to retirement you may be, **18 Wealth Lessons That Will Transform Your Thinking** is worth reading again and again.

This book would be an excellent gift for any young person starting or about to start out on a career. If they take the lessons seriously and apply them...when retirement comes, regardless of what they do for a living – butcher, baker or candlestick maker – they could be set for life, with a retirement portfolio valued well into seven figures.

—**Russell Martino**

Master Copywriter, Marketing Expert

PREFACE

Why on earth would I write my sixth book? Fair question. After three-plus decades in the wealth management business, after reading hundreds of book on wealth and attending countless seminars, roundtables, and conferences, I've come to the conclusion that the vast majority of Americans are simply not paying attention.

Look around. Millions of folks are watching hours of TikTok videos and YouTube, and messaging each other with cute memes while standing in line for a cup of five-dollar coffee. Hello! Does anybody see a problem here? What happened to America's work ethic and history of self-reliance? In the past year or two, millions have chosen to stay home and watch TV reruns and play video games while collecting pandemic-related government benefits instead of looking for a job and providing their employer with an honest day's work. Still others might have begun a business, yet chose not to. In a word, we're talking about choice.

I wrote this book to remind those who are interested that there is an unmistakable way—a specific blueprint—that helps ensure a superior financial outcome. Does this book guarantee you will be rich? Obviously not. I sat down and considered some of the same things that must have run through Napoleon Hill's head when Andrew Carnegie purportedly commissioned him in 1908 to create a compendium of the laws of success and wealth. My hope is to spark something deep inside of you so you will pursue your highest and best goals. *I want you to have the freedom to live like you want to live and even be able to help others and improve humanity along the way.* I deliberately designed this book to be interactive. Why? Because if you read the book, put it back on the shelf, and take no notes or action, you'll have achieved nothing. The choice is yours.

INTRODUCTION

On the following pages, I have attempted to synthesize and present wisdom I gained from my very successful mentors and my own personal experiences. I will highlight wealth magnates such as Jim Rohn, Brian Tracy, Dan Kennedy, Lee Milteer, Jay Abraham, and others. Most of this wisdom is from *in-person learning*—sometimes sitting in a Mastermind event or a conference with Brian, Dan, or Lee for probably hundreds of hours. Distilled are lessons that I wish were taught in high school and college but weren't.

I never had the opportunity to meet the late great Jim Rohn, but I am grateful for the lessons he imparted to me in books and recorded audio. And I also spent *years* listening to Brian Tracy and Dan Kennedy during my daily commute. **Every day and on every trip**, my "Drive-Time University" was in session. I made wealth my major. I studied it like an architectural student studies drafting or a computer science major explores robotics or artificial intelligence. I studied wealth. I studied money.

Over the years, I have refined my understanding of wealth. And now I want to challenge your beliefs about money and wealth.

Here's what I believe: **The primary reason to pursue wealth is autonomy**—*the ability to do what you want . . . when you want . . . with whom you want . . . where you want . . . and on the terms you want.* These important aspects of wealth were taught to me by Dan Kennedy, and for that I owe him a debt of gratitude.

This is what you want to achieve—and you want to achieve it as quickly as possible. Some call it a *safe harbor position*. Some call it **independence** or **freedom**.

WHAT YOU WON'T FIND IN THIS BOOK

I want you to know right up front what is *not* in this book. I don't want you to read nine paragraphs and then be disappointed that I'm not teaching you investment basics. There are far too many books out there that accomplish that just fine. And there will be no mention of the following:

- Investment recommendations
- Stock tips
- Merger and acquisitions analyses
- Market analyses
- Cryptocurrency strategies
- Strategies to start your own business

So let's get back to what this book *is* about—***autonomy***. Attaining wealth is much more than just being able to do what you want, when you want. It's about self-discovery. It's about spending time with family and friends rather than trading hours for dollars. <u>It's about providing financial security to yourself and those you love.</u> It's about being able to be involved in your kids' or grandkids' educational choices.

There are very few things in this world that compare to being able to *write the check* that makes all the difference to someone you care about. Does that take wealth? It does—but don't immediately say you'll never be wealthy. Most people don't believe that's possible or even consider the idea of becoming wealthy. It just doesn't cross their minds.

Poor people rarely buy books with "wealth" in the title, just one of the many reasons they stay poor.

—DAN KENNEDY

Author, *No B.S. Wealth Attraction for Entrepreneurs: The Ultimate No Holds Barred Kick Butt Take No Prisoners Guide to Really Getting Rich*

Becoming wealthy does not mean you must be a greedy and self-serving, but it does mean you must look around you and not do the things you see everyone else doing. Why? Probably because ***the overwhelming majority of Americans will never, ever attain wealth.*** You must attain a heightened self-awareness, something the population at large has failed miserably to do. And once you understand this, **action** is the next step. I never learned this in college.

This one important idea—that wealth is attainable—has perhaps eluded you for years. Maybe you have never considered that wealth is positively correlated with a willingness to take on greater responsibility in life, at work, in your business. Get ready to ask some tough questions that will often lead to remarkable breakthroughs. It's time to get serious about what you are capable of accomplishing.

At the conclusion of each section, you will find an area to write down the strategies you will use to implement the lesson. Take advantage of this while your mind is focused on each lesson. Later, transcribe your notes and work to create your own wealth blueprint.

Are you wondering if I have the qualifications, credentials, and moral authority to present this material to you? Should you trust me to teach you what you've never been taught? The short answer is **yes**. And here's why:

- I'm the child of an entrepreneur.
- I have more than 36 years of experience designing and managing retirement portfolios.

- I have written five books, four of them on retirement planning and one on marketing.

- I'm a former Senior Vice President and Senior Investment Management Consultant with Morgan Stanley Wealth Management.

- I hold the Chartered Retirement Planning Counselor^{SM} designation from the College for Financial Planning.

- I have been featured and interviewed by WTOP News, *USA Today*, Fox Business, Fiduciary News, *U.S. News & World Report*, and dozens more.

Simply put, I manage retirement wealth, and I've worked with hundreds of "from scratch " multi-millionaires.

Make no mistake, the wealth lessons I will share with you were probably not offered to you in high school, in college, or by your parents. Unless you were lucky enough to be raised in an entrepreneurial family like I was, this information will be eye opening, life altering, and probably disconcerting. <u>You might be disturbed by what you read in these pages, if so, this book and its lessons are not for you</u>. My dad was an entrepreneur who was never content with average. He always looked for ways to improve, to produce, to be better, and to teach his children that being a productive member of society carried with it great rewards.

I learned these lessons through painstaking personal experiences and observations. Each lesson has been instrumental in my journey toward wealth and autonomy. I opened my first IRA account with a $600 contribution since I did not have $2,000 to make a full year's contribution. And then I ended up with a negative net worth thanks to credit card debt. All that is behind me now, but I remember them like it was yesterday. And why is it behind me now? <u>Because I believed that wealth was possible, and I wasn't afraid to put that belief into action</u>. Then I learned from the best.

I found it is absolutely critical to regularly communicate with a core group of *from-scratch multi-millionaires* who enjoy idea sharing and celebrating the success of others. Unlike many I have met during my career, they are not jealous of the accomplishments of others; rather, they are supportive and eager to assist.

> *It's better to hang out with people better than you.*
> *Pick out associates whose behavior is better than*
> *yours and you'll drift in that direction.*
>
> **—WARREN BUFFET**

This elite group of individuals doesn't apologize for achievement, wealth, or their beautiful home or luxury car. They dine on the fruits of their labors while caring for others and supporting causes they deeply care about. They understand that the more they help people, the more their businesses will thrive and the more they can help others. These individuals don't gather, study, and work so they can boast about their millions. They do what they do so they can enjoy *freedom* and *autonomy*—ideals that *appear* to be out of reach for a majority of the population. Here's the difference—these individuals have the willingness, persistence, and inner drive to pursue excellence. They don't quit. They thrive.

If possible, surround yourself with these types of individuals as I have. This kind of camaraderie is important. They teach you, they mentor you, and they encourage you. And they help you maintain your sanity in a world where wealth, the pursuit of wealth, and autonomy are often frowned upon.

It's easy to understand these ideas when we look at self-made, from-scratch **billionaire Sara Blakely** who started the hugely successful SPANX brand with an idea, a pair of scissors, and $5,000.

Was she an expert in fashion? *No.*

Was she just another employee at Disney World? *Yes.*

Was she a two-time miserable failure after taking the LSAT to try to get into law school? *Yes.*

Did she spend seven years selling fax machines by cold-calling and knocking on doors? *Yes.*

Was she an improbable billionaire? Yes!

Her secret?

She took action.

She wasn't timid!

In the rest of this book, we'll look at what from-scratch millionaires (billionaires?)—people who have attained wealth—have in common. One common characteristic is the propensity to hire experts when they lack a needed skill set. Another characteristic is making decisions that many are unwilling to make. And then it's following those decisions with consistent, purposeful action.

These individuals have an *abundance mindset*. It's not about collecting expensive toys to impress their friends. It's about independence and the ability to have choices—choices that many do not have.

You build wealth by taking action.

Consider, why would you engineer a life that does not allow for financial independence? Why would you work for 40 years only to see Social Security payments make up the majority of your retirement income? This is not a dress rehearsal. This is it, and you'd better get it right the first time. So let's get on with it. Let's look at **18 Wealth Lessons** that will transform your thinking and change your life.

WEALTH LESSON

1

Look Around – What Do You See?

L ook around at what everyone else is doing—**and don't do that**. Why? Simple. I believe <u>the majority is always wrong, especially about money.</u> Need proof? Why is it that the majority of Americans worry about money their entire lives? Why is it that they never seem to have enough? Why are they in debt?

Why can't they seem to save enough for their retirement? Why do they spend more than they earn? Why don't they ever read books on wealth, money, debt, or finance?

You must adopt the mindset that others are unwilling to adopt. (For more on this subject, see my book *The Mindset of Retirement Success: 7 Strategies to Change Your Life*). Those who are financially unsuccessful are generally unwilling or unable to do what the successful do. When I was in my 20s, I spent time in the library (pre-Internet) while my colleagues enjoyed happy hour. They knocked back beer after beer while I devoured books on wealth, debt, and finance. I learned about commercial real estate, REITs, common stocks, and bonds. I read about gold and silver. I became conversant in the language of money. My "friends"—well, some became alcoholics with beer bellies who continued to line up every night for half-price drinks and free appetizers during happy hour. Sadly, wealth has eluded many of them.

Navigate your own pathway to wealth. Find out what it takes to have financial freedom. That means you study. If you're a lawyer, you've studied law in depth. If you're a physician, you've read and digested medicine. I'm asking you to study wealth. You cannot become wealthy without understanding wealth. Sure, Uncle Bill and Aunt Doris might leave you five million dollars, but I wouldn't bet on it.

Don't fall into the trap of telling yourself that since you work all day, you deserve to come home at night and relax, play with the kids, and watch some TV. Your spouse (if you have one) will most likely not begrudge your spending 45 minutes each evening learning how to bring more money into your household. Here's how studying 45 minutes each night translates:

- 315 minutes each week (there are 10,080 minutes in a week).
- That's 0.03% (three-tenths of a percent!) of your week.

Do you think you can swing that? If you're really motivated like I was, double that to 90 minutes each night, and speed up your learning curve.

Keep in mind that this will not put you on par with Warren Buffet or Elon Musk, but it will allow you to understand financial concepts that were foreign to you a short while ago. The more you understand, the better position you may be in to make financially sound decisions.

What strategies will I use to implement this lesson?

1._____

_____

_____

_____

2. _____

_____

_____

_____

3. _____

_____

_____

_____

4. _____

_____

_____

_____

5. _____

_____

_____

_____

Name a successful person and the trait you admire most in them.

_____

_____

_____

What will you do to implement that trait in your own life?

_____

_____

_____

WEALTH LESSON

2

Habits

Habits are the things you repeatedly, consistently, and purposefully think and do. I want you to think about effective and efficient methods of focusing your thoughts, behaviors, and actions in a decisive manner.

As I look around, I see many people with their heads buried in their phones watching endless TikTok videos of cute kittens and puppies or funny memes. It brings back memories of my early 20s when I lived in Flushing Queens (New York City) and watched six or seven ball games over the weekend, glued to the TV for 20 or more hours and accomplishing nothing. Boy, was I ever in my comfort zone, but what I needed was a radical departure from my comfort zone.

My mentor, Brian Tracy, the personal development, wealth, and success teacher, is fond of saying, "*One of the very worst uses of time is to do something very well that need not be done at all.*" Cute kittens and puppies and my couch-potato, sports-watching days are great examples of that—precious time flushed down the toilet.

A colleague of mine stands in line each morning at Starbucks, eagerly waiting for a supersized 24-ounce cup of something that appears to be a chocolate milkshake, although he calls it coffee. This is his ingrained habit, and he never misses a day. He forks over a five-dollar bill and tells the barista to keep the change. That's $4.45 for *something that has to do with coffee* and a 55-cent tip. This $35 weekly expense won't break his bank, but think of how that $1,825 annual expense might be repurposed to wealth-building. Also, imagine the amount of sugar he is consuming!

I also have an ingrained coffee habit. I periodically purchase a two-pound bag of Mocha Java from my favorite roasting facility, make the brew at home, put it in a to-go cup, and enjoy it on my way to the office. A little creamer and no sugar, and I'm on my way. The cost: a mere 50 cents a cup. I'm not cheap—far from it.

But think about it. My colleague spends 10 times what I do and wastes precious time standing in line seven days a week waiting to hand cash to a multi-billion-dollar corporation. He loves sugar; I love adding dividend-paying common stocks to my portfolio. It comes down to the choices you make.

Let's do an interesting exercise. Use the page at the end of this Wealth Lesson to write down all your money habits—you know, all the ones that put money in and take money out of your pockets. I'm not asking you to create a budget, although that might be a wonderful use of your time. I'm asking you to dig deeply into your brain and write down all the money and wealth stuff crammed between your ears. Next, write down your beliefs about money. Think what you might have heard at the top of the stairs when you were little and eavesdropping on your parents' private conversations. Did you hear anything like these?

- Money doesn't grow on trees.
- I'm already working as hard as I can.
- We can't afford that.
- Money is tight right now.
- Maybe next year.
- We don't have enough money.
- I need to work more overtime.

As Tony Robbins is fond of saying, you most likely have a lot of junk in that attic (your brain). Consider a mental yard sale, and toss some mental junk to the curb. Most likely, some of those ingrained beliefs may be holding you back. They may be the root cause—*or at least a contributing cause*—of unproductive money behaviors.

MY MONEY HABITS

My money habits that put money in:

_____

_____

My money habits that take money out:

_____

_____

What I believe about money:

_____

_____

What strategies will I use to implement good money habits?

_____

_____

WEALTH LESSON

3

Self-Defeating Behaviors

The road to wealth and personal autonomy contains more potholes than a downtown street in New York City. Shiny objects abound—new electronic gadgets, $1,200 cell phones, and more places to sink your hard-earned cash than ever before. And how you behave as you navigate nearly constant distractions may well determine where you end up. Successful wealth creation demands an *abundance mindset*, and make no mistake, that mindset is not common today.

My friend Lee Milteer often speaks of this and has created a concise list of 10 of *the most common self-defeating behaviors*. With 100% of the credit to Lee Milteer, here is her list:

1. Procrastination
2. Getting involved with the wrong people
3. Playing it safe
4. Focusing on what others are doing wrong
5. Not learning from your mistakes
6. Having unrealistic expectations
7. Trying to take care of everybody
8. Being envious of others
9. Letting fear run your life
10. Dismissing new opportunities, sources of information, new perspectives before you have given them the time and attention to evaluate them

This list doesn't apply only to a wealth-creation mindset. Lee's lessons also apply to your business life. Do you see a common thread? *It's all about behavior.*

Behavior is what separates the wealthy from the unwealthy. It is not about skin color, sexual orientation, what side of the tracks you grew up on, or who your parents are. It is about what you do with your time and what you allow into your world and into your mind.

> *Wealth is the product of man's*
> *capacity to think.*
>
> —FRANCISCO D'ANCONIA
> **Ayn Rand,** *Atlas Shrugged*

WHAT ARE MY TOP 5 SELF-DEFEATING BEHAVIORS (from Lee Milteer's list)?

1._____

_____

_____

2._____

_____

_____

3._____

_____

_____

4. _____

_____

_____

5. _____

_____

_____

What strategies will I use to fix these self-defeating behaviors?

1. _____

_____

_____

2. _____

_____

_____

3. _____

_____

_____

4. _____

_____

_____

5. _____

_____

_____

WEALTH LESSON

4

Intention

A t first blush, many would think there's no common thread among wealthy people. But consider for a moment; might it take industriousness, focus, intelligence, persistence, or hard work to create and maintain wealth? Are wealthy people all skinny, Catholic, tall, male, or polite? Actually, people with deep pockets come from every walk of life. But there may be one thing that separates those who attain wealth from those who do not—*conscious intent*. Some refer to it as mindset.

And that leads us to their common thread. They are all **behavior-based—they are intentional**. Wealth has everything to do with your behaviors and the decisions you make.

While I have never met a real-life billionaire, I have met many wealthy people. And none of them have impressed me more than Nido Qubein. I had the good fortune to attend a conference where Qubein was the keynote speaker.

For those unfamiliar with the name, this remarkable man came to this country from Lebanon at age 17 with $50 in his pocket and the ability to speak only a few words of English. What he did have, though, instilled by his widowed mother, were values and principles.

Today, Qubein is president of High Point University in North Carolina. An accomplished entrepreneur, although not a billionaire, he serves as Chairman of Great Harvest Bread Company and sits on the boards of BB&T bank (now Truist after the merger with SunTrust) and La-Z-Boy Furniture Company. Seldom do you find a president of a college who has not risen through the ranks of academia. For a successful businessman and entrepreneur to head a college is virtually unheard of. *He is a master of communication, motivation, and personal development.*

Qubein is also a professional speaker and motivational expert. His books and programs have sold millions of copies worldwide. He was inducted into the International Speaker Hall of Fame, earned the Horatio Alger Award for Distinguished Americans, and was Citizen of the Year and Philanthropist of the Year in his home city of High Point, North Carolina.

More than anyone I have ever met, Qubein is a person of significance. My guess is that he has accumulated a vast fortune, which *seems to be a byproduct* of becoming a phenomenal communicator and a person of significance. Everything he has become is because of his behavior and the decisions he has made. There's a lesson here...

Remember, Qubein came here as a poor, legal immigrant with no English skills. He worked relentlessly to achieve success. To quote the late-great Jim Rohn, *"Become a millionaire not for the million dollars, but for what it will make of you to achieve it."* It seems that Rohn may have been speaking about Qubein.

Who do you know (or know of) who is significant because of their...

Industriousness: _____

_____

_____

Focus: _____

_____

_____

Intelligence: _____

_____

_____

Persistence: _____

_____

_____

Hard work: _____

_____

_____

Impact on others (or the world): _____

_____

_____

What strategies will I use to become more significant?

1._____

_____

_____

2._____

_____

_____

3._____

_____

_____

4._____

_____

_____

5._____

_____

_____

WEALTH LESSON

5

Willingness

Far too many people are not *willing* to do what is necessary to achieve wealth. Many believe there are very few millionaires and that those people are lucky or somehow chosen at birth for great wealth. They don't have a belief or a willingness to accept that it is possible for them. Nothing could be further from the truth.

Here are some examples of individuals <u>with a burning desire</u>

to succeed—people who have no fancy degrees and no business experience.

- **Tom Monaghan** had no mentors, no money, and virtually no business experience. Yet at age 23, he opened his
  Domino's Pizza restaurant and had sales of $99 in the first
  week. Today, Domino's Pizza has thousands of stores and
  revenues in the billions.
- **Dave Thomas** left high school in the 10th grade. He
  worked at a lunch counter at age 12 and later became a
  cook in the Army. In 1969, he opened his first Wendy's
  hamburger restaurant and grew the concept to thousands
  of stores and billions in revenues.
- **Quentin Tarantino** dropped out of high school. It was
  not the surest or quickest path to Hollywood fame, but
  Reservoir Dogs and *Pulp Fiction* helped make him rich
  and famous.
- **Joe Polish** received an "F" in a small business course at his
  community college and a "C" in principles of marketing.
  In time, he owned a small and failing carpet-cleaning business and was dead broke. Yet, the Creator of *Piranha Marketing* and *The Genius Network* is one of the most astute
  marketers on the planet with millions in the bank.

None of these entrepreneurs were born with a silver spoon in
their mouths. They lacked a college degree and displayed none

of the outward signs of outsized success. Each was focused and did not give up on their dreams. They had the burning desire— the willingness—to succeed, and that is exactly what they did. Along the way—slowly at first and then building over time—each amassed large personal net worth, and none of it was by accident. The takeaway? **The economy doesn't determine your destiny; you do. In other words, the economy is between your ears. It doesn't get more personal than that.**

RATE YOUR DESIRE TO SUCCEED

On a scale of 1 to 5, rate your current desire to succeed (1=no desire; 5=burning desire).

1 2 3 4 5

Do you believe you can become wealthy?

YES   MAYBE   PROBABLY NOT   NO

What am I willing to do to increase my desire to succeed? to change my belief about achieving wealth?

1._____

_____

_____

_____

2._____

_____

_____

_____

3._____

_____

_____

_____

4._____

_____

_____

_____

5._____

_____

_____

_____

WEALTH LESSON

6

Understand What You Can and Can't Control

Let's start with a short list of what you can and can't control:

- Market returns
- Interest rates

- Tax policy
- Inflation rate
- Longevity
- Spending habits
- Asset allocation

You either have control of these factors or not. For example, it is fairly evident that you have little or no control over market returns, interest rates, the rate of taxation, or inflation.

You have limited control over your longevity, or the length of your life, but you can certainly influence it by eating healthy foods and getting plenty of rest. You can engage in regular exercise and avoid smoking. If heart disease or some dreaded sickness runs in your family, you may have less ability to influence those variables.

But you do have control over your spending habits and your methods of asset allocation, as well as the types of accounts that hold these assets. Asset allocation refers to the percentage of your assets you place in various types of investments. You may choose to be an aggressive investor, allocating a majority of your assets to real estate or equities, or you may choose to be a more balanced investor, allocating your assets to a mixture of stocks, bonds, precious metals, cash and perhaps real estate.

The types of investments you place in a variety of accounts (taxable accounts versus tax-favored accounts such as IRAs,

SEP-IRAs, HSAs, or Roth IRAs) may also have a major influence on the after-tax returns you enjoy in retirement.

Corollaries of asset allocation are *portfolio diversification* and *risk mitigation*. There are many strategies to diversify a portfolio. Some methods are effective, and others are less so. Your goal is to own a portfolio of assets that complement each other.

Keep in mind that as you approach retirement, your goal is to own a portfolio of assets sufficiently diversified to help mute major market declines. Remember, there are declines in real estate as well as the stock market, and you don't need a worldwide pandemic to see the next one coming. You are not looking for the next big score by having 50% of your portfolio in gambling stocks, biotechnology, or the energy sector.

You will also want to mitigate risk in your portfolio but in conjunction with your desired returns. For example, while fixed-income assets (e.g., bonds and CDs) are usually viewed as conservative in nature, a heavier allocation of fixed-income assets in your portfolio might actually expose you to a higher risk of outliving your assets, primarily due to the allocation's inability to keep pace with inflation. Here in the U.S. the inflation rate rose to 6.8% in 2021, it's highest since 1982. As I finished writing this in February 2022, the inflation rate reached 7.5%. Meanwhile, a one year C.D. (Certificate of Deposit) earns approximately one half of one percent.

Until you take control of your own life someone else will.

—JACK WELCH

Industrialist, CEO, Author

How can I have more control?

List 5 things you do *not* have control of:

1._____

2._____

3._____

4._____

5._____

List 5 things you have *limited* control of:

6._____

7._____

8._____

9._____

10._____

For each one, strategize how you can specifically gain more control:

1._____

_____

_____

2._____

_____

_____

3._____

_____

_____

4._____

_____

_____

5._____

_____

_____

6. _____

_____

_____

7. _____

_____

_____

8. _____

_____

_____

9. _____

_____

_____

10. _____

_____

_____

WEALTH LESSON

7

Urgency

I vividly remember sitting in a gigantic arena years ago, somewhere on the outskirts of Chicago. I was attending my first Tony Robbins event (you can save your giggles—he ignited a burning desire in me to achieve success), and he said something that stuck with me to this day. I can repeat it even now—from memory. *When would NOW be a good time?*

In a word, the genius of his message was *urgency*. He said to disregard what unproductive friends and colleagues are doing and chart a personal path to success. He told us to ignore all the bad news the media hoists on us every day and to triumph despite the headwinds we encounter.

At times it feels like a stake is being driven through the heart of our nation's economy—inflation, a never-ending pandemic, government overreach, geopolitical infighting, and more. Yes, I'm worried about our borders, about Russia, about China. What rational, informed person wouldn't be? We live in a dangerous world. Yet we can't hide our heads in the sand.

Without a sense of urgency, desire loses its value.

—JIM ROHN

The truth is that *we create our own reality* by the questions we ask ourselves and by our thoughts, decisions, behaviors, beliefs, habits, courage, rituals, and willingness to take action. You probably won't manifest a new wealth reality by watching endless reruns of *NCIS* or *All in the Family*, or by reading the newspaper for hours. Time must be put to good use. Procrastination must be replaced with urgency. Fear and self-doubt must be replaced with decisiveness and action.

Many people while away hours on Facebook, Instagram, Twitter and Tik Tok yet say they are too busy to meet with an advisor and begin the wealth-planning process. These same folks have time for vacations—the ones they pay for with a credit card. *I'm too busy*, they say.

Remember . . .

Wealth is created by a sense of urgency and deliberate choice.

My personal path to success (my own reality)

In the graph below, ignore the "bad news" of our reality at the bottom. Across the top, add deliberate choices that will lead to your success.

PERSONAL PATH TO SUCCESS					
My Deliberate Choices for Success					
↑	↑	↑	↑	↑	
↓	↓	↓	↓	↓	
The "Bad News" market	Inflation	Pandemic	Government overreach	Media	Stock

And it's about URGENCY . . . so WHEN will you implement these choices (create a timeline)?

_____

_____

_____

_____

_____

_____

_____

8

Get Comfortable Being Uncomfortable

You may find that focusing on achieving wealth is uncomfortable. Many people ask why. I have found no better answer than the one offered by my mentor, Dan

Kennedy, who is often referred to as "the Millionaire Maker." In his own words:

> Not only does discomfort precede the attraction of wealth, actually for most highly successful entrepreneurs, there's a continuous and consistent level of discomfort and frustration. I think anybody that is a high achiever finds themselves surrounded by low achievers, and so the natural dichotomy of trying to get slow people to move faster because you're moving faster creates a lot of frustration.
>
> Fundamentally, the discomfort for a lot of people comes from changing their philosophy, their strategy and their behavior to be attractive to wealth. So, long ingrained habits of thought and behavior have to be changed, and when they really are changed, it's almost like flipping switches on the wall in that the results come so fast and furious.
>
> Getting to the point that you can believe for example, and honestly believe, that there's an infinite amount of money and not a finite amount of money that you can honestly believe that every adversity of personal or economic or societal or in your industry actually offers greater opportunity. Getting to the point that you are totally focused on leverage rather than on work for dollars

can be a real uncomfortable thing for a lot of people. It's the shedding of long held deeply ingrained beliefs that are really tough for people.

Kennedy also stated:

So, if you look at just about anybody who is consistently attracting wealth and consistently experiencing growth in both their business and personal finances, you will find to a great degree <u>that they're willing to do things that other people aren't willing to do</u> that the vast majority of people choose very temporary and transitory satisfactions rather than enduring some difficult or some discomfort or some sacrifice for a bigger and better gain.

That says it all. Now, read it again.

Get comfortable being uncomfortable

List some of your long-ingrained negative thoughts and behaviors about wealth.

1._____

_____

2._____

_____

3. _____

_____

4. _____

_____

5. _____

_____

Now . . . replace them with positive beliefs about success and wealth.

1. _____

_____

2. _____

_____

3. _____

_____

4. _____

_____

5. _____

_____

9

Set Wealth Goals

You would be surprised at how few people set wealth goals. Stated differently, <u>the majority of Americans do not set wealth goals</u>. And that is a very good reason why you should. Remember, the majority of people are always wrong about money. Look no further than the vast amount of Americans who continue to worry about money no matter what the economy is doing.

The major reason for setting goals is not the achievement of the goals; it is to compel you to become the person it takes to achieve them.

—JIM ROHN

It's not my place to tell you what your wealth goal should be. For some, it might be $1 million. For others, it might be $5 million or more. You alone decide. When you set a wealth goal, you are in effect creating a target to aim for. Without a target, just where do you suppose you are aiming? You will encounter obstacles and setbacks, which are to be expected and planned for. Still, many people manage to succeed in spite of them. You want to count yourself among them.

My friend Lee Milteer says it this way:

Your focus and goals need to be crystal clear and you should have back up strategies for accountability.

Planning for wealth is not a set-it-and-forget-it exercise. View it as living and breathing the strategies that you continually amend, tweak, and use in your daily life. If you think you can create a draft plan, stick it in a drawer, and consider yourself all set, you're sadly mistaken. A better idea might be to put it on your refrigerator door with a magnet and read it whenever you get something to drink or prepare a meal.

Life has no limitations, except the ones you make.

—LES BROWN

It's like going to your doctor for a regular checkup. You want to make sure all your vital systems are in order and that you're free of disease. In the same way, you need to check and recheck your wealth plan to make sure you are on the proper trajectory. It's also like a plane traveling from New York to San Diego; it will go off course due to atmospheric conditions such as air pressure, storm clouds, and wind speed. They combine to knock the plane off its intended flight path. However, the flight computers and the pilots act to bring the plane back on course toward its intended destination, and it lands precisely on the proper runway at the San Diego airport.

Your wealth plan will be knocked off course. Your investment portfolios will have to deal with periods of low interest rates, market downturns, periods of rising interest rates, and actions by the Federal Reserve. If you own real estate, you will inevitably have periods where your rental property is empty with no one paying you rent. Yet your mortgage and taxes will still be draining funds from your bank account whether or not you have a tenant.

Add to those a pandemic crisis, the US debt, the inability of Congress and the President to agree on anything, never-ending fighting in the Middle East, and tensions with Iran, North Korea,

Russia, and China. All these "happenings" act to disrupt the plans you have put in place. Some are "noise" and should be ignored. Others are important signposts you must discuss, consider, and, when appropriate, act on.

As I created my own wealth goals, I spent countless hours reading Jay Abraham's books. His ability to create wealth in a wide variety of businesses is nothing short of breathtaking. Here is his philosophy summed up in his own words:

I have a very simple philosophy on life. You shouldn't steal from yourself. If you're going to commit your life to an enterprise, wealth creation, the security and the financial well-being of your family... and if other people—your staff, your team, your employees, your vendors—are going to commit their lives to you, you owe it to yourself and to everyone else to get the highest and best results. You should never accept a fraction of the yield when with the same effort or less, the same people or fewer, the same time or less, the same capital or less, the same opportunity cost or less, can deliver so much more to you currently, and perpetually.

MY PERSONAL WEALTH GOALS

My crystal-clear wealth goals with target dates:

_____

_____

Target Date: _____

_____

_____

Target Date: _____

_____

_____

Target Date: _____

_____

_____

Target Date: _____

_____

_____

Target Date: _____

What strategies will you use to implement these goals and meet
your target dates?

_____

_____

_____

_____

_____

_____

WEALTH LESSON

10

Decide

I read somewhere a long time ago that most people never *decide to be wealthy*. I thought it an odd thing. Who <u>decides</u> to be wealthy? Evidently, a lot of folks do. The article said that most folks are not wealthy because they never decided to be. Imagine that!

I could decide to be an NBA superstar or an astronaut. A lot of good that would do me. Yet <u>there is great power in a decision</u>.

Sylvester Stallone, star of the *Rocky* movie franchise, decided he could beat Clubber Lang, Apollo Creed, and the Giant Russian to become the champion.

But make no mistake. Often a prime reason individuals don't **decide** to improve their life—become financially independent and wealthy—is that they become too comfortable with their current position in life. They tell themselves, *Well, it's not that bad. I have a decent car, my apartment is okay, I got a 2% cost of living salary increase, and I've got some money in the bank.*

But there is a huge difference in *getting by* and *thriving.* I vividly remember a time in college when I could pay my phone bill or buy beer, but not both. I was very annoyed with myself, and no, I won't tell you which one I chose.

> *Don't worry about failures, worry about the*
> *chances you miss when you don't even try.*
>
> **—JACK CANFIELD**
> **Co-author,** *Chicken Soup for the Soul*

As my college experience was winding down, I reflected on all the classes I had taken, all the credits I had stacked up, and all the reports I had written. And nowhere in there were any guidelines, tips, rules, or recommendations on how to become wealthy.

I came away from college with a lot of useless information that I would never use in my career.

Years later I was browsing in a bookshop in the personal development aisle, and two books caught my eye. By the way, the reason I was in the personal development aisle was because I recognized that I could use some more developing.

The first book was *Think and Grow Rich* by Napoleon Hill. The second was *7 Strategies for Wealth & Happiness* by Jim Rohn. Each of these books spoke about the power of decision and its ability to alter the trajectory of your life. I ***decided*** to purchase the books, forgo watching five football games that weekend, and immerse myself in those books. I'm glad I did—they provided me a blueprint for success and wealth that I've followed for decades.

*I **DECIDE** to do the following to give myself more **time** and **opportunity** to become successful and wealthy*

_____

_____

_____

_____

_____

List at least two things that keep you from improving your life (especially financial independence and wealth):

1._____

_____

_____

2._____

_____

_____

WEALTH LESSON

11

Avoid Stupid

A friend of mine related the following story:

> Our 30-year-old daughter brought her boyfriend to spend the week at our Colorado home. They enjoyed skiing and all the outdoor activities of the season. I noted that the fellow, let's call him Ed, was constantly checking

his phone. Didn't matter if we were driving somewhere, in the middle of a conversation, sharing a meal or on the ski lift, he kept checking his phone.

Unable to ignore his rude behavior, I asked why he was glued to his phone. He responded that he was checking the price of the Brazilian real versus the US dollar. When I asked why this was important to him, he responded that most of the stocks he owned were denominated in that currency and that he didn't realize it at the time of purchase. He had failed to consider the added risk of currency fluctuations on his holdings.

To say this fellow failed to consider a host of investment risks is an understatement. I chalk it up as **stupid**. He took action without sufficient investigation or research. I sure wouldn't want this guy managing my daughter's investments.

Beware of stupid mistakes. They can derail even the best of plans. Going off *"half-cocked"* (Merriam-Webster defines this as *to do or say something without preparing for it or thinking about it*), and the resulting poor outcomes often result in tremendous delays in reaching your goals.

And remember—don't be so arrogant or self-righteous that you believe you can't make a stupid mistake. I've seen scores of stupid decisions from seemingly bright folks, including dozens with a PhD. To think it can't happen to you is both shortsighted and unrealistic.

Case in point; I recall a discussion with a seemingly very bright young lady with three degree's from an Ivy League University. When I reviewed the employer sponsored retirement plan statement she provided me, I discovered that although her employer generously provided three percent in matching funds, she was only contributing one percent, effectively not receiving free matching funds. When I brought this to her attention, her only response was "oh!"

> *Life is hard. It's harder if you're stupid.*
>
> **—John Wayne**

Okay, let's get painfully honest – What stupid mistakes have I made in my lifetime (that I wish I could go back and change)?

Yes, I was stupid when I . . .

1. _____

_____

2. _____

_____

3. _____

_____

4. _____

_____

5. _____

_____

Now, how will I go forward and make better choices?

_____

_____

_____

_____

_____

_____

_____

_____

_____

12

Hire Expertise You Don't Possess

I f you don't have expertise in a certain area, hire a professional. I'm not talking about getting financial advice from your brother-in-law (unless he's a financial planner, a CPA, or a multi-millionaire). We all know that family means well, but your brother-in-law or your roofing contractor is not the person you should choose to help you create a wealth plan. Call that roofing contractor when you have a roofing issue, but he's the last one you should call for advice as critical as your financial independence.

I am a great believer in seeking out credentialed expertise. I lead a retirement wealth planning team with decades of experience, and we have helped scores of investors build wealth so they can enjoy a financially independent retirement. Building an advisory team around you to act as a sounding board for your ideas and help you plan may be one of the single-most important decisions you make.

You might be a heck of a physician, plumber, crane operator, software engineer, or retail store owner, but do you have the skill set to craft a wealth accumulation plan?

Crafting a wealth plan is not a walk in the park. You don't *wing it*. You don't go to Tik Tok or Instagram for guidance. You study and ask questions—lots of them. You seek out professionals who have helped people like you attain their goals. If you are married, have three children, or own a shoe store, don't hire an advisor who works primarily with government workers who are single. You want someone—and preferably a team—who has massive experience working with people like you.

What professionals do I need to contact – the ones who will help me reach my financial goals?

Professional area (CPA, financial planner, lawyer, etc.):

_____

Name / Firm: _____

Contact Info: _____

_____

_____

Professional area (CPA, financial planner, lawyer, etc.):

_____

Name / Firm: _____

Contact Info: _____

_____

_____

Professional area (CPA, financial planner, lawyer, etc.):

_____

Name / Firm: _____

Contact Info: _____

_____

_____

13

Automate and Set Reminders

Your life is complicated enough without trying to remember every facet of your wealth strategy. When possible, automate your decision-making process, and then set periodic reminders.

For example, many investors contribute to an employer-sponsored retirement plan such as a 403(b) or 401(k) plan. These types of plans automatically pull a portion of your pay and invest it in your retirement plan account. You don't have to think about it or do it yourself.

And what about setting reminders? They will prompt you to periodically increase your contribution level. I have spoken with many seemingly smart folks who have not upped their contribution level in years because they never thought about it. They commonly respond, "Oh yeah. I can do that."

In addition to retirement plan contributions, you may want to consider a strategy I used for decades. If I were paid on the 15th of each month, the very next day I invested a set percentage of my after-tax pay into an investment. It became an automatic response. I get paid—I invest the very next day. I did that month after month, year after year.

Some call this type of plan *dollar cost averaging*. You periodically put a set amount into an investment over a period of months or years. Don't trust yourself to remember to do this. Set reminders to invest a certain percentage at regular intervals.

I will set reminders to periodically increase contributions to my investment and retirement plans

Plan: _____

Reminder date: _____

Amount or percentage of increase: _____

Plan: _____

Reminder date: _____

Amount or percentage of increase: _____

Plan: _____

Reminder date: _____

Amount or percentage of increase: _____

Plan: _____

Reminder date: _____

Amount or percentage of increase: _____

Plan: _____

Reminder date: _____

Amount or percentage of increase: _____

WEALTH LESSON

14

Debt—the Good, the Bad and the Ugly

I never learned in school that there is good debt and bad debt. Imagine if I had discovered at the age of 19 that the shiny new MasterCard in my wallet was a harbinger of bad debt. I saw the little plastic rectangle as a badge of honor and the window to newfound freedom. No longer would I have to worry that I didn't have cash to make a purchase. I could always *pay later*.

And I had a lot of company. Many around me also had shiny new credit cards, and we all went into debt together. Some of them were over-achievers and collected many shiny new credit cards. They went into more debt than anyone else.

Let me share a short story with you. Early in my career, I took on a client I should have never worked with. She was the sister of a secretary who worked at my firm. This woman was in her early 30s and held a mid-level managerial position at a large department store. She earned almost $45,000 per year.

During my discovery interview with her, this well-spoken and somewhat chatty young lady fell silent when I asked if she had any debt. I knew there was no home mortgage since she shared a rental apartment with her sister. It turned out that she had a debt load that was almost twice her annual salary. I was astounded. She had applied for and received credit cards from almost every major bank I could name, and she had charge cards from darn near every department store in town.

One of her primary goals was to begin to work on her debt situation. She agreed it was getting out of hand. Over the following weeks, I crafted a strategy that she agreed she could live with. She would pay off the cards with the highest interest rates first—and at the time, the interest rates on these cards were 14% to 21%. We made solid progress and whittled down the number of cards from 16 to 7. But her old habit slowly reared its ugly head again after she fell in love and wanted to shower her man with presents. She ran up her credit cards again, and that is when we parted ways.

Some people have emotional triggers that cause them to overeat, smoke, or drink. Some create art or write, and others, well, they spend money they don't have.

—RODGER A. FRIEDMAN

By the way, according to Northwestern Mutual's September 2021 Planning & Progress Study, US adults ages 18 and older carry an average debt of $23,325 outside of their mortgages. So if you refuse to consider yourself average, you have a choice to make. And yes, it all comes down to the choices you make.

At the opposite end of the spectrum is good debt—such as taking on debt to purchase your primary residence or income-producing real estate. Think smart debt—prudently considered and acted upon in an intelligent manner. Smart debt can be a wonderful stepping-stone to building wealth. I know people with five or more mortgages on single-family properties they rent to responsible renters whose monthly payments pay down the mortgage balances. These investments allow them to build equity over time while providing important tax benefits associated with investment real estate.

My debt – the good, the bad, and the ugly

My good debt:

Financial institution: _____

Balance due: _____

Financial institution: _____

Balance due: _____

Financial institution: _____

Balance due: _____

My bad debt:

Financial institution: _____

Balance due: _____

Financial institution: _____

Balance due: _____

Financial institution: _____

Balance due: _____

What is my strategy to get rid of my bad debt?

_____

_____

_____

_____

15

Spend Less Than You Earn

The widespread use of credit has allowed millions of Americans to spend more than they earn. They're happy knowing they don't have to pay for things now and that it can wait until later. Banks charge high rates of interest on the unpaid balances, and folks seem all too happy to pay it.

There are **three important elements** to spending less than you earn:

1. After you pay all your monthly bills, you should still have some money.
2. Do something intelligent with those leftover funds. Allowing the excess dollars to pile up in a checking account at near zero interest rates will not create the outcome you are after. The important thing is to intelligently and methodically put the funds to work in a consistent manner.
3. Rein in your desire for instant gratification. It's called **discipline**.

Think of saving money each month as a monthly bill. Make it your number-one financial priority. Some of the most successful and wealthy Americans made it a point to save 15% to 20% of their income—and then they invest those funds wisely. They view their required savings as a bill that must be paid each month, just like a utility bill.

The three elements of spending less than you earn are not easy to master. They are difficult because there is a near constant temptation to spend. Walk down any street with storefront window displays, open any magazine or newspaper, or search the Internet, and you will see ads everywhere that encourage you to spend money. Television is peppered with commercials for new cars, cell phones, appliances, and backyard swimming pools. Controlling your desire to spend is hard because humans are *hardwired* to want things. If you ever doubt that, look at children and their desire for *things*.

Think . . . spend less . . . invest more.

Am I spending more than I earn?

a.   **My monthly net income:**

$_____

b.   **My monthly bills:**

$_____

c.   **Approx. monthly expenses (food, gas, entertainment):**

$_____

Subtract b. and c. from a. (leftover money):

$_____

I commit to investing (10%, 15%, 20%, 25%, 30%) (circle one) of my income each month (and pay it consistently as though it were a monthly bill).

Describe how you will strategically make that happen.

_____

_____

_____

_____

_____

_____

_____

_____

WEALTH LESSON

16

Be Tax-Aware

When I was a young teenager, my dad put me on the payroll at his shop, Norton's Laundry. The store was located in Times Square in New York City. This was no normal laundry operation. My dad had inherited the business from his parents. He started out with one washing machine and grew it to a 14,000-square-foot facility with dozens of washing machines and 48 employees.

One day Dad pulled me aside and informed me that he had placed me on the company's payroll and that going forward I would receive a paycheck instead of cash. I guess my dad was intent on teaching me about the tax code. Why else would he put a 14-year-old on the *ADP* payroll system?

Regardless of his reason, I worked like a sweating dog loading and unloading 100-pound washing machines, folding hundreds of draperies, and pressing shirts, pants, and other assorted clothing items. By the end of a typical 12-hour day, I was beat. The only bright spot was every Friday at 6:00 p.m. when I lined up with the other workers to receive a pay envelope.

When I opened my first envelope with a check inside instead of cash, I read every line of the attached check stub. Remember, this was New York City in 1970, and tax rates were quite different than they are today. I was stunned when I saw that the IRS, New York State, New York City, and *someone named FICA* had taken nearly 35% of my money. That check stub, my first ever, smacked me in the head like a bag of silver dollars. Said more elegantly, that was the day I became tax-aware.

Fast forward to building your wealth today. What do you need to be aware of? Well, how about this short list for starters:

- Find and work with a competent CPA.

- Understand the difference between long-term and short-term capital gains.
- Understand the difference between mutual funds and exchange traded funds (ETFs).
- Gain a basic knowledge of tax-free municipal bonds.
- Know the benefits of real estate investing.
- Be aware of 1099s and K-1 tax reporting basics.
- Learn the differences between C corporations, S corporations, LLCs (limited liability companies), and sole proprietorships.

While there are many more tax issues to be aware of, this will be a good beginning. I have known people who have paid massive unnecessary tax bills simply because they never thought to educate themselves or ask for competent tax advice from a tax professional.

(P.S. In my life, I have never met a financially poor accountant.)

My tax know-how – what I need to know

I am ...

_____ an employee

_____ an employer

_____ a sole proprietor

_____ an S corporation

_____   a C corporation

_____   an LLC (limited liability company)

_____   other

What percentage of my income goes to federal taxes?

_____%

What percentage of my income goes to state taxes (if applicable)?

_____%

What are my strategies to reduce the taxes I am paying?

_____

_____

_____

_____

_____

_____

_____

_____

_____

17

The Difference between Philosophy, Strategy, and Tactics

S tanding in line at the Apple Store can be an eye-open-
ing experience. While I was waiting behind a group of
Millennials, I overheard a conversation about *getting
rich* and how they were going to do it. Evidently, the plan was
to buy cryptocurrencies. That's it—no philosophy about what
they wanted to accomplish, no strategy or long-term plan. They
jumped right to tactics and decided which vehicle would deliver
their desired results.

The development of a *personal wealth philosophy* is deeply
emotional and has been instrumental in my own wealth journey.
Understanding how wealth moves about, what attracts wealth,
and what repels it has been critical to my understanding of accumulating capital. From there, I developed realistic strategies,
accumulated necessary skills, and formed important networks to
enhance the probability of a successful outcome.

The most important part of my philosophy is the realization
that wealth is not a zero sum game. Global wealth is unlimited.
What you or I accumulate does not take anything away from your
neighbor down the block. Your neighbors, your friends, and your
fellow citizens do not have less because you have more. Wealth is
created by focused and sustained effort.

I read a story years ago about wealth that is appropriate here.
Pretend that money—wealth—is like the ocean. You can go to
the shore with a teaspoon or a tanker truck and take as much as

you wish. The ocean doesn't care. Most folks are timid—content to take a teaspoon or two. It takes guts and foresight to get hold of a tanker truck and park it at the shoreline. Remember, there are no shortages of tanker trucks or teaspoons.

And what will you do with all that "water" (wealth)? It depends on your wealth philosophy, which is deeply personal. A friend of mine built a wildly successful enterprise and now has the ability to make very large charitable gifts to causes he cares deeply about. That is what motivates him to rise at 6:00 a.m. and work until dusk. Writing a six-figure check to a local charity inspires him more than a fancy car or sailboat.

Another friend now has the ability to annually fund a scholarship that sends kids from broken homes to college. That is what is important to her since she came from a broken home and saw firsthand the obstacles and challenges these kids face.

Whatever your philosophy, whatever your reason to attain wealth, most likely it will be deeply personal. A shiny car doesn't require a philosophy. The wealthiest folks I know are also the most charitable. They don't advertise it, but they send enormous amount of money to causes that are important to them. This, in large part, is what the pursuit of wealth may be about. To fund causes you feel strongly about. **The more money you have, the more you can help others.**

Surplus wealth is a sacred trust, which its possessor is bound to administer in his lifetime for the good of the community.

—ANDREW CARNEGIE

Now let's consider what strategies you can implement to create the wealth you desire. Will you attend business school, obtain a professional degree, or acquire skills that are in high demand? Will you start your own business or become a real estate investor? The choices are as endless as your own imagination. Spend a lot of time on this, and don't jump quickly to tactics as the *Apple Store Millennials* did.

True wealth is not rushed, and neither is the planning.

Tactics should never precede strategy. Take a page from Dan Kennedy's playbook. Let's say your strategy is to create a sales letter to increase sales of your new whiz bang widget. The **sales letter** is the strategy. How you implement that strategy is the tactic. Will you mail the letter? Send it by Fed-Ex? Post a video sales letter (VSL) on a website? Will you place the letter on a 12x16 post-card? These are all examples of what tactics you will use to implement your strategy. But the strategy came first.

MY WEALTH PHILOSOPHIES, STRATEGIES, AND TACTICS

What are my personal wealth philosophies?

_____

_____

_____

What are my wealth strategies (skills I need, a network, etc.)?

_____

_____

_____

What tactics will help me accomplish my wealth goals (sales letter, social media ad, etc.)?

_____

_____

_____

What motivates me (why do I really want to attain wealth)?

_____

_____

_____

18

Clarity

Remember Wealth Lesson #10—*Decide*? It talked about having the ability to make a definitive statement about what you want, what you want to achieve, the amount of money you want to make, and the ultimate purpose of that money.

Related to that concept is *clarity*—**your ability to be crystal clear about what you want and why you want it**. What are your expectations of the future and the reasons for those expectations?

What do you anticipate for your income, your net worth, how you will live, and where you will live? All these require clarity of thought.

> *If you get clear on the what, the how will be taken care of.*
>
> —JACK CANFIELD
>
> Author, *The Success Principles: How to Get from Where You Are to Where You Want to Be*

You don't meander to prosperity, you don't fall into a million dollars, and you don't accidently become wealthy. Serendipity will not come to the rescue.

Years ago, I wrote the following in my private journal:

- I want to marry an intelligent and beautiful woman.
- I want to have children—one boy and one girl.
- I want my kids to have the best education possible.
- I want a big, beautiful home with a large backyard for the kids to play in.
- I want my family to be healthy and happy.
- I don't want my wife to have to work.
- I want to be debt-free.
- I never ever want to worry about money.
- I want to have an enjoyable career where I make a difference.

Everything I wrote down has come to pass. It wasn't easy, and it wasn't quick. But it happened.

<u>Clarity requires you to expend mental energy</u>, something that appears to be in short supply today. Many would rather stay home and be happy receiving government checks while they watch reruns of their favorite TV shows.

Wealth and success require that you show up and do something. But like traveling from Kansas City to Orlando, it's best to plan your trip before backing out of the driveway. Your plans may not pan out, but the planning process is often indispensible. Clarity of thought requires that you take in all available information and make practical decisions—decisions that often need to be adjusted as additional information becomes available.

My intent in writing this book was to spur your thinking and perhaps give you ideas you haven't considered. If you take away one or more actionable ideas, I have met my objective.

LET'S MAKE THIS CRYSTAL CLEAR . . .

What are my expectations for the future (in 5 years, 10 years, 15 years . . . 40 years)?

_____

_____

What do I anticipate my annual income will be (in 5 years, 10 years, 15 years . . . 40 years)?

_____

_____

What about my future net worth?

_____

_____

_____

Where will I be living?

_____

_____

_____

How will I be living?

_____

_____

FINAL WORDS

I want to express my gratitude to my mentors; Dan Kennedy, Jay Abraham, Brian Tracy, Lee Milteer, Gary Halbert, Joe Polish, Jim Rohn and others that have provided so much of what I have learned that has allowed me to be where I am today. Thank you all.

MY STORY

As a six-year-old in 1962, I remember waiting at my grandparents' apartment for my grandpa to show up on Thanksgiving Day with a big, golden turkey. My grandpa was a kindly old man with thinning gray hair and a twinkle in his eye. He was completely devoted to our family. My grandparents owned a small paint supply store on the east side of Manhattan, which he and my grandmother had run for decades. They didn't make much money, but it paid the rent for their apartment.

As I played with my toys, my dad and uncles gazed out the window, waiting for Grandpa. Suddenly, they started shouting and ran out of the apartment. My grandpa, who had been walking down the street, had just suffered a massive heart attack, collapsed, and died on the sidewalk. The turkey was scattered all around him. I saw all this unfold through the upstairs window and remember gripping the arm of the plastic-covered couch with all my strength, trying to remain steady while all around me everyone was shouting and screaming.

Shortly after Grandpa died, Grandma was forced to close the paint store because she was unable to run it by herself. Every Saturday morning after that, my dad sat down at a small mahogany table in the living room and wrote Grandma a check for $115. My grandma did not have enough income to survive, and the check allowed her to remain in her apartment where she and Grandpa had lived for 50 years. My father wrote those checks because he loved her and did not want to see her struggle.

Her Social Security check was not enough for her to live on. Grandma had already seen a lot of adversity in her life, and she didn't need more. She had fled Poland at the beginning of the Nazi occupation and was very lucky to reach America. She lost her country to Hitler, lost her husband to a heart attack, and lost her livelihood when she was forced to close the paint store. I watched Dad hand Grandma that check week after week, year after year.

Even at that young age, I felt it was wrong for someone to have to accept money every week from their child. It left a huge impression on me and motivates me to this day. I grew up, went to college, and studied political science and economics.

After college, I took a job as an internal auditor with a giant brokerage firm in New York. My responsibilities included interviewing stockbrokers from all over the country to make sure they complied with the regulations of our company, the Securities and Exchange Commission, and other government agencies. That job led to a second defining moment that helped focus and change the direction of my life.

I was interviewing a young stockbroker who was about 30 years old. He was a cocky fellow, anxious to get back to trading his clients' accounts, and he was clearly annoyed at me, the operations guy from New York who was interrupting his day. I noticed that he wouldn't make eye contact with me as I questioned him. As we made our way through the interview, it quickly became clear that he was lying to me.

He sat there explaining his trading strategy, telling me how he was performing such a great service for his clients. It was dawning on me that he was churning his clients' accounts, trading excessively to enrich himself at their expense. He was the sort of stockbroker I was trained to spot, document, and report to my superiors.

As I listened to him lie, I remained outwardly calm although I was seething inside. I wanted to scream at him for staining the honor of our firm, for acting dishonestly, and for lying to his clients. How many regulations and laws had he broken just to put another buck in his own pocket? He was hurting the very people who trusted him with their financial lives.

I decided then and there that I would learn to manage retirement funds, but unlike that broker, I would do it ethically and with heart. I would guide clients on how to structure their finances for a successful and financially rewarding retirement. I would make a difference in their lives so they would not have to rely on their children to make ends meet as my grandma did all those years ago.

That is why I do what I do. That is why I am passionate and focused on helping family leaders make the best decisions possible for a successful and independent retirement.

*   *   *

Rodger Alan Friedman leads a credentialed advisory team that offers families across the nation a holistic, comprehensive, planning-based approach to wealth management and retirement planning.

The team focuses on assisting a limited number of families in developing written wealth-building strategies, retirement income strategies, and structuring their planning and investments to help them meet their goals.

The team has many years of experience working with entrepreneurial family leaders who are 50 and older, have achieved financial success, and need their expertise to create additional strategies that help preserve their wealth and maintain their desired standard of living.

AND HERE IS WHAT THE LAWYERS ALWAYS ASK ME TO SAY.

This material is protected by copyright, ©2022, written by Rodger Alan Friedman, Chartered Retirement Planning Counselor.

Although I have mentioned deferring and eliminating taxes in this book, please understand that I AM NOT GIVING TAX ADVICE, and you should visit with a tax professional for personal tax advice.

This information does not purport to be a complete description of the securities, markets, or developments referred to in this material. The information has been obtained from sources considered to be reliable, but we do not guarantee that the foregoing material is accurate or complete. Any information is not a complete summary or statement of all available data necessary for making an investment decision and does not constitute a recommendation. Any opinions are those of Rodger A. Friedman.

This information is not intended as a solicitation or an offer to buy or sell any security referred to herein. Keep in mind that there is no assurance that our recommendations or strategies will ultimately be successful or profitable or protect against a loss. There may also be the potential for missed growth opportunities that may occur after the sale of an investment. Recommendations, specific investments, or strategies discussed may not be suitable for all investors. Past performance may not be indicative of future results. You should discuss any tax or legal matters with the appropriate professional.

This publication is designed to provide accurate and authoritative information in regard to the subject matter covered. It is provided with the understanding that the publisher is not engaged in rendering legal, accounting, or other professional services. If legal advice or other expert assistance is required, the services of a competent professional person should be sought. This information is not intended as a solicitation or an offer to buy or sell any security referred to herein. Keep in mind that there is no assurance that our recommendations or strategies will ultimately be successful or profitable or protect against loss. There may also be the potential for missed growth opportunities that may occur after the sale of an investment. Recommendations, specific investments, or strategies discussed may not be suitable for all investors. Past performance may not be indicative of future results. You should discuss any tax or legal matters with the appropriate professional.

During his life, Michael Maurer was in "my business," someone who spent countless hours learning best practices, attending hundreds of workshops, conferences, webinars, and roundtables. He was certified five times over. He was fond of helping others move up and happily shared his ideas, knowledge, and opinions.

His sharing was not confined to business. He was charitable with both his money and <u>his time</u>, helping kids with sports and organizing and supporting leagues and events. Oh yeah, he was also as smart as a whip and never stopped learning. To him, class was always in session.

Michael Maurer was my branch manager at Smith Barney for years. He was the smartest and most helpful manager I ever had the good fortune to work with. After the merger with Morgan Stanley, Mike, along with Jim Gold and Hy Saporta founded Steward Partners Global Advisory.

He instilled in others that success is accomplished by a methodical and painstaking implementation of sound strategies year after year, not the sudden winning of a lottery. He succumbed to illness at 51 years old.

I keep this picture on my desk, to remind me of my friend and mentor and the outsized impact he had on my life. I am forever grateful to my friend Michael Maurer.

ACKNOWLEDGMENTS

I would like to express my gratitude to Sue Vander Hook, my wonderful copy editor and story partner, for polishing my writings with needed corrections and organization so they can be published. Sue has edited hundreds of my articles as well as several of my books. Most important, she can spell, something I never learned to do. Having written more than a dozen books, Sue understands proper structure and grammar. I owe her a debt of gratitude that far exceeds payment for value received. Other than her decision to live in one of the coldest parts of the country, I trust her judgment implicitly.

In my teenage years, I sometimes wrote in my journals about my dad. I used adjectives for him such as focused, persistent, organized, and methodical. Andrew Friedman sparked my lifelong pursuit of financial freedom and autonomy. Watching him grow a small laundromat to a successful enterprise that employed dozens of workers was a continuous lesson in the pursuit of excellence. Yet he always made sure to leave time for family, friends, and relaxation. Being able to enjoy the fruits of his labor was the reason he built a thriving business. Why else should we work long hours and risk our capital than to reap the rewards created by our hard work and dedication?

One of Dad's biggest lessons was what to do when you don't know how to do something. The successful person adds that to their list of things they have to learn. The unsuccessful person says, "I don't know how to do that." Dad learned to do things and drove that point home as I watched him learn to repair machines in the laundry, knowing he could figure it out quickly instead of wasting a day's output waiting for a repairman to arrive. I have spent the last two decades learning how to do things I didn't know how to do. Thanks, Dad . . .

Made in the USA
Columbia, SC
23 June 2024

37220735R00068